The ESSENTIALS® of
REGISTERED TRADEMARK

ADVANCED ACCOUNTING I

William D. Keller, Ed.D.
Professor of Accounting
Ferris State University, Big Rapids, Michigan

D1319521

This book ~~covers the usual course outline~~ of Advanced Accounting I. For additional topics, see *"THE ESSENTIALS OF ADVANCED ACCOUNTING II."*

Research and Education Association
61 Ethel Road West
Piscataway, New Jersey 08854

THE ESSENTIALS ®
OF ADVANCED ACCOUNTING I

Printed in the United States of America

Library of Congress Catalog Card Number 96-67812

International Standard Book Number 0-87891-692-X

ESSENTIALS is a registered trademark of Research & Education Association, Piscataway, New Jersey 08854

WHAT "THE ESSENTIALS" WILL DO FOR YOU

This book is a review and study guide. It is comprehensive and it is concise.

It helps in preparing for exams, in doing homework, and remains a handy reference source at all times.

It condenses the vast amount of detail characteristic of the subject matter and summarizes the **essentials** of the field.

It will thus save hours of study and preparation time.

The book provides quick access to the important principles, equations, theorems, and concepts in the field.

Materials needed for exams can be reviewed in summary form – eliminating the need to read and re-read many pages of textbook and class notes. The summaries will even tend to bring detail to mind that had been previously read or noted.

This "ESSENTIALS" book has been prepared by an expert in the field, and has been carefully reviewed to assure accuracy and maximum usefulness.

Dr. Max Fogiel
Program Director

CONTENTS

CHAPTER 1

SOLE PROPRIETORSHIPS

1.1 Business Entities

In regard to business entities, the business is separate from the owner as far as accounting is concerned.

Sources of Equities:

1. Net Assets contributed by owners
2. Income earned but not yet distributed by owners

Reporting of Capital in a Single Proprietorship—in one capital account.

No distinction is made between investments and undistributed earnings.

Increase in Owner's Equity comes from increased investment or plowed-back profits.

Decrease in Equities comes from withdrawals by owner or losses in running the business.

1.2 Proprietary Theory

From the owner's point of view, there is no separation between the business and the natural person (owner).

1.3 Entity Theory

The business is entirely separate from the owner.

1.4 Fund Theory

Under the Fund Theory, assets are restricted to specific uses only. This theory usually applies to estates, trusts, and not-for-profit organizations.

1.5 Conversion from Cash to Accrual Basis of Accounting

In order to convert to accrual basis, the beginning and ending balances of the unrecorded balance sheet accounts must be known and used in the conversion.

EXAMPLE

In order to convert the Cash Basis Sales Revenue to the Accrual Basis Sales Revenue, start with Cash Basis Sales Revenue, deduct beginning Accounts Receivable, then add ending Accounts Receivable to get Accrual Basis Sales Revenue.

1.6 Income Tax Reporting for a Sole Proprietorship

Sole proprietorships, as such, pay no income taxes.

Net income of a sole proprietorship is taxed on the sole proprietor's personal tax return.

1.7 Personal Financial Statements

Industry Audit Guide, Audits of Personal Financial Statements, by the American Institute of Certified Public Accountants, 1968, required personal financial statements to use *Cost Values* and suggested that *Current Values Be Presented as Supplementary Information.*

Statement of Position Covering the Accounting and Financial Reporting for Personal Financial Statements, also issued by the American Institute of Certified Public Accountants in 1982, requires assets and liabilities to be reported at their *Estimated Current Values.* It allows the presentation of historical cost values of assets and liabilities as supplementary information.

1. Lenders want current values in order to determine the debt-paying ability of the person.
2. Current values are needed for income-tax planning.
3. Current value financial information is needed by candidates for public office.

1.8 Statements of Financial Condition

Statements of Financial Condition must be prepared on the Accrual Basis, according to Generally Accepted Accounting Principles.

Usually the assets and liabilities are more important than income in these statements.

In the personal Statement of Financial Condition, the assets and liabilities of a personally owned business could be placed in footnotes.

A Statement of Financial Condition is similar to a balance sheet, except that assets and liabilities reflect market prices, not cost prices.

1.9 Disclosure Requirements

Footnotes of Statements of Financial Condition should give information such as:

1. Descriptions of Intangible assets and their Useful Lives
2. Descriptions of the maturities, interest rates, and collateral for receivables and debt
3. Methods used to compute estimated income taxes on unrealized gains and losses
4. Methods used to determine current values of assets

1.9.1 Statement of Changes in Net Worth

The Statement of Changes in Net Worth usually accompanies the Statement of Financial Condition for an individual or married couple and gives increases and decreases in net worth during the year, both realized and unrealized. A sample follows:

William and Betty Keller
Statement of Changes in Net Worth
For Year Ended December 31, 1992

Realized Increases in Net Worth:

Income from Keller Hardware Store	$30,000	
Salary of Betty Keller	15,000	
Dividends from Marketable Securities	3,000	
Total Realized Increases		$48,000

Realized Decreases in Net Worth:

Income Taxes	13,000	
Real Estate Taxes	12,000	
Interest Expense	3,500	
Personal Expenditures	18,000	
Total Realized Decreases		(46,500)
Net Realized Increase in Net Worth		1,500

Unrealized Increases in Net Worth:

Keller's Hardware Store	3,200	
Life Insurance	400	
Residence	6,000	
Total Unrealized Increases		9,600

Unrealized Decreases in Net Worth:

Marketable Securities	2,800		
Estimated Income Taxes on the Differences Between the Estimated Current Values of Assets and the Estimated Current Amounts of Liabilities and Their Tax Bases	1,200		
Total Unrealized Decreases		(4,000)	
Net Unrealized Increase in Net Worth			5,600
Net Increase in Net Worth			7,100
Net Worth at the Beginning of the Year			103,000
Net Worth at the End of the Year			110,100

Summary

1. An entity can be a person, a business or a nonbusiness enterprise.

2. The equity is the assets minus liabilities.

3. Income statements are not usually prepared for sole proprietorships because of the mix of personal and business affairs.

Chapter One Review Questions

1. Which is the simplest type of business organization?

Sole Proprietorship

2. Are sole proprietorships a separate legal entity?

No. They have no legal life of their own, apart from the owner.

3. Are sole proprietorships a separate accounting entity?

Yes, they should be. Each business should have its own set of books.

4. If one looks at his business as being a part of himself or herself, what is this termed?

Proprietary Theory.

5. If we tend to think of the business as apart from ourselves, what is this termed?

Entity Theory.

6. If the various assets of the business are set aside for specific purposes, what is this termed?

Fund Theory.

7. Why is it necessary to convert assets of a single-proprietorship business from the cash basis to the accrual basis?

Generally accepted accounting principles require reporting by the accrual basis, and many single-proprietorship businesses keep their books on the cash basis.

8. How do single-proprietorship businesses compare with corporations as far as paying income taxes?

Single-proprietorships, as such, pay no income taxes. Their earnings are added to the income of the owner. Corporations, as such, do pay income taxes.

9. According to the latest generally accepted accounting principles, how are assets to be recorded on Statements of Financial Condition?

At estimated current values, not at cost.

10. Is a Statement of Changes in Net Worth required to go along with a Statement of Financial Condition?

No, this is not required by generally accepted accounting principles, but it is recommended.

CHAPTER 2

PARTNERSHIPS IN GENERAL

2.1 Definition of Partnership

A partnership is an association of two or more persons to carry on, as co-owners, a business for profit.

2.2 Number and Extent of Partnerships in the United States

In 1982, there were over 1.5 million partnerships in the United States, as compared to 2.9 million corporations.

The number of partners in the U.S. is about 10 million.

2.3 Reasons for Organizing Partnerships

1. To cut expenses
2. To increase services
3. To add expertise
4. For professional people, such as accountants, lawyers, and medical doctors, to become partners with their fellow professionals

2.4 Advantages of Partnerships

Ease of Formation—Only an oral agreement is necessary, but the agreement should be in writing to protect the individual partners.

The Partnership itself pays no income taxes, although it must file an annual tax return. Any partnership income must be apportioned among or between the partners, and each partner pays taxes on his or her portion of the partnership profits individually.

2.5 Disadvantages of Partnerships

Unlimited Liability—Any partner can be held personally liable for all debts of the business.

Mutual Agency—Each partner has the right to incur liabilities in the name of the partnership. This gives each partner the ability, if he or she desires, to run up huge debts for the partnership.

Difficult to attract large amounts of ownership capital. Potential investors fear that their money can be lost too easily.

2.6 Limited Partnerships

Limited Partnerships allow people to invest money and retain a limited liability status. These limited partners, in case of bankruptcy, would lose only the amounts invested in the partnership and no more. Even in limited partnerships, however, there must be at least one general partner with unlimited liability.

2.7 Uniform Partnership Act

The Uniform Partnership Act is a straightforward legal statement showing a proper method for setting up partnerships. This was approved in 1914 and has now been adopted by 44 states. Many firms operate in more than one state, so uniformity of law is important.

Uniform Limited Partnership Act

The Uniform Limited Partnership Act is also a straightforward legal statement showing the proper method for setting up limited partnerships. Approved in 1916 and adopted in 47 states.

2.7.1 Articles of Partnership

Articles of Partnership is a legal convenant, oral or written, which governs the operation of a partnership.

1. Names and addresses of each partner
2. Location of the business

3. Nature or type of business
4. Rights and responsibilities of each partner
5. Specific method by which profits and losses are to be allocated
6. Periodic withdrawal of assets by each partner
7. Methods of admitting new partners
8. Methods of arbitrating partner disputes
9. Method of settling a partner's share in the business upon withdrawal, retirement, or death

2.7.2 Evaluation of a Partnership

Partnerships have some freedom from government control, with few regulatory or reporting requirements. They have few organizational costs.

Partnerships are often able to attract services of persons with different abilities, wealth, and interests.

Partnerships lack continuity, because a partnership ends with the death, insanity, or withdrawal of a partner. Also an entirely new partnership is formed with the admission of another partner.

2.7.3 The Partnership Agreement

The most important agreements between partners are changes in partners, and dissolution of the partnership. Partners should agree on the division of responsibilities, and the amount of time and effort that each is to contribute.

Pro and Con — Partnerships can attract more capital and people with perhaps more skills than do single proprietorships, but trouble often comes in deciding among the partners, as to who is boss.

Capital Accounts — The main difference in accounting for partnerships as different from accounting for single proprietorships, is the treatment of partners' capital accounts. Each partner has his or her own capital account.

2.7.4 Income Share Plans

Profit and Loss Sharing Arrangements

In the ratio of partners' capital account balances on a particular date, or in the ratio of average capital account balances during the year

Allowing interest on partners' capital account balances and dividing the remaining net income or loss in a specified ratio

Allowing salaries to partners and dividing the remaining net income or loss in a specified ratio

Bonus to managing partner based on income

Allowing salaries to partners, allowing interest on capital account balances, and dividing the remaining net income or loss in a specified ratio

Equally or in some other ratio

2.8 Financial Statements of a Partnership

Financial Statements of a partnership include Income Allocation Schedule, Statement of Partners' Capital Balances, Income Statement, Balance Sheet, and Statement of Cash Flows.

EXAMPLE

Income Allocation Schedule

**HAMMOND-BROWN PARTNERSHIP
INCOME ALLOCATION SCHEDULE
FOR YEAR ENDED DECEMBER 31, 19x5**

	Hammond	Brown	Total
Salary	$10,000	$15,000	$25,000
Interest:			
8% × $130,000 for Hammond	10,400		10,400
8% × $152,000 for Brown		12,160	12,160
Total Salary and Interest	$20,400	$27,160	$47,560
Remainder Shared Equally	1,180	1,180	2,360
Allocation of Income	$21,580	$28,340	$49,920

9

EXAMPLE

Statement of Partners' Capital Balances

HAMMOND-BROWN PARTNERSHIP
STATEMENT OF PARTNERS' CAPITAL BALANCES
FOR YEAR ENDED DECEMBER 31, 19x5

	Hammond	Brown	Total
Capital, January 1, 19x5	$130,000	$152,000	$282,000
Add: Additional Investments	22,000		22,000
Net Income, according to allocation	21,580	28,340	49,920
Subtotal	$173,580	$180,340	$353,920
Less: Withdrawals	−15,000	−10,000	−25,000
Capital, December 31, 19x5	$158,580	$170,340	$328,920

2.9 Partnership Operations

For the most part, partnership operations are the same as other forms of business operating in the same line, except:

Personal expenses of partners should not be included as business expenses of the partnership — Personal expenses of partners that are paid for with partnership funds should be debited to partner's drawing accounts.

The Revenue and Expense Summary account should be closed out, moving the net profit or loss to the partners' capital accounts according to the partnership agreement, using an Income Allocation Schedule and a Statement of Partners' Capital Balances.

Chapter Two Review Questions

1. *How many partners can join a business firm?*
   There is no top limit of partners in a firm. The bottom limit is two.

2. *Are there more partnerships or corporations in the United States?*
   More corporations.

3. *Do partnerships have to file annual federal income tax returns?*

Yes

4. Why does the federal government exempt partnerships from paying federal income taxes?

The Federal Government collects the partnership income tax through the Individual Partners' tax returns.

5. What is the purpose of the partnership federal income tax return?

The Federal Government compares the partnership return with the individual returns of the partners to be sure that each partner is including his or her full share of the partnership income in his or her return.

6. Why do some people want to become limited partners?

They have money to invest in the partnership but do not want the responsibility of managing the business, nor do they want to pay more than their individual investment in case of bankruptcy.

7. Are articles of partnership set up by the state?

No. They are agreed to by the partners setting up the partnership, but they should be based on the Uniform Partnership Act passed by most state legislatures.

8. What is the main difference between accounting for a single-proprietorship business and accounting for a partnership business?

In a single proprietorship, only the owner has a capital and a drawing account. In a partnership, each partner has a capital and a drawing account.

9. In a partnership, how are profits divided among the partners?

According to the agreement called The Articles of Partnership.

10. Should personal expenses of a partner be listed in the partnership income statement?

No. These should be moved to the debit side of the partner's drawing account.

CHAPTER 3

PARTNERSHIP CHANGES IN OWNERSHIP

3.1 Tangible and Intangible Assets

Purchase of an Existing Partner's Interest

Let us say that Partners A and B share profits and losses equally.

Partners A and B have capital account balances of $60,000 each.

C purchases all of B partnership interest for $67,500, making payment directly to B.

The following entry will be made on the partnership books:

Partner B. Capital	60,000	
Partner C, Capital		60,000

Note: The $67,500 that C pays B is not recorded on the partnership books.

Investing in an Existing Partnership; No Bonus or Goodwill

Let us say that Partners A and B share profits and losses equally.

Partners A and B have capital account balances of $60,000 each.

C agrees to contribute $60,000 cash for a $1/3$ interest in the partnership.

The following entry will be made on the partnership books:

Cash	60,000	
Partner C, Capital		60,000

Investing in an Existing Partnership; Bonus to Old Partners

Let us say that Partners A and B share profits and losses equally.

Partners A and B have capital account balances of $60,000 each.

C agrees to contribute $90,000 cash for a $1/3$ interest in the partnership.

The following entry will be made on the partnership books:

Cash	90,000	
Partner C, Capital		70,000
Partner A, Capital		10,000
Partner B, Capital		10,000

(In the new partnership, there will be a total capital of $210,000 — the $60,000 of Partner A, the $60,000 of Partner B, plus the $90,000 cash contributed by New Partner C. One-third of $210,000 is $70,000, which will be credited to New Partner C's account. The remaining $20,000 bonus will be divided equally between the old partners since in the old partnership they divided profits and losses equally.)

Investing in an Existing Partnership; Bonus to New Partner

Let us say that partners A and B share profits and losses equally.

Partners A and B have capital account balances of $60,000 each.

C agrees to contribute only $30,000 cash for a $1/3$ interest in the partnership.

The following entry will be made on the partnership books:

Cash	30,000	
Partner A, Capital	10,000	
Partner B, Capital	10,000	
Partner C, Capital		50,000

(In the new partnership, there will be total capital of $150,000 — the $60,000 of Partner A in the old partnership, the $60,000 of Partner B in the old partnership, and the $30,000 cash contributed by New Partner C. C agrees to contribute only $30,000 for a $1/3$ interest in the new partnership. So Cash is debited for the $30,000 received from New Partner C. However C's capital account is credited for ⅓ of $150,000, or $50,000. The difference of $20,000 is borne equally by Old Partners A and B, so their accounts are debited for $10,000 each.)

Investing in an Existing Partnership; Goodwill to New Partner

Let us say that Partners A and B share profits and losses equally.

Partners A and B have capital account balances of $60,000 each.

C agrees to contribute only $30,000 cash for a ⅓ interest in the partnership.

A and B refuse to have their capital balances cut.

The $120,000 (A's investment of $60,000 plus B's investment of $60,000) will equal ⅔ of the capital of the new partnership. Thus the total capital of the new partnership is $120,000 divided by ⅔ or $180,000. C's share (⅓ of $180,000) will be $60,000. The difference between C's capital ($60,000) and C's cash investment ($30,000) is the goodwill ($60,000 − $30,000 = $30,000). The entry would be:

Cash	30,000	
Goodwill	30,000	
Partner C, Capital		60,000

(In the new partnership, there will be total capital of $150,000 — the $60,000 of Partner A in the old partnership, the $60,000 of Partner B in the old partnership, and the $30,000 cash contributed by the New Partner C. C agrees to contribute only $30,000 for a ⅓ interest in the new partnership. So Cash is debited for the $30,000 received from New Partner C. However C's capital account is credited for ⅓ of $180,000, or $60,000. Since the old partners refuse to have their capital accounts decreased, the difference of $30,000 is debited to goodwill.

Investing in an Existing Partnership; Goodwill to Old Partners

Let us say that Partners A and B share profits and losses equally.

Partners A and B have capital account balances of $60,000 each.

C agrees to contribute $80,000 cash for a ⅓ interest in the partnership.

14

C insists that his Capital Account be credited for the full $80,000 that he is contributing.

The following entry will be made on the partnership books:

Cash	80,000	
Partner C, Capital		80,000
Goodwill	40,000	
Partner A, Capital		20,000
Partner B, Capital		20,000

(In the new partnership, there will be total capital of $200,000 — the $60,000 of Partner A, the $60,000 of Partner B, plus the $80,000 cash contributed by New Partner C. Since Partner C is investing $80,000 for a $1/3$ share of the business, this implies that the business must really be worth $240,000 — $80,000 divided by $1/3$ = $240,000. Subtracting the actual worth of the business, $200,000, from the implied worth of the business, $240,000, we get goodwill of $40,000. Since in the old partnership the profits and losses are divided equally, each of the old partners' capital accounts is credited for $20,000.)

Revaluation of Assets

When a new partner is admitted, the partners may agree to revalue assets to market value at the time the new partner is admitted. Let us say the partners agree to increase the Land Account by $10,000 and that Partners A and B share profits and losses equally.

The entry would be:

Land	10,000	
Partner A, Capital		5,000
Partner B, Capital		5,000

Withdrawal of a Partner; No Bonus or Goodwill

Let us say that Partner C, with a capital balance of $80,000, withdraws and takes the money.

The entry would be:

15

Partner C, Capital	80,000	
Cash		80,000

Withdrawal of a Partner; Bonus to Withdrawing Partner

Let us say that Partner C, with a capital balance of $80,000, withdraws, but all the partners agree to let this partner take $100,000.

The entry would be:

Partner C, Capital	80,000	
Partner B, Capital	10,000	
Partner A, Capital	10,000	
Cash		100,000

(The extra gift of $20,000 to the retiring partner would be divided between the remaining partners according to the ratio of profit or loss division previously agreed to in the articles of partnership—in this case equally.)

Withdrawal of a Partner; Goodwill Going to the Withdrawing Partner

Let us say that Partner C, with a capital balance of $80,000, withdraws and all the partners agree to let this partner take $100,000 but the other partners don't want their capital accounts decreased.

The entry would be:

Partner C, Capital	80,000	
Goodwill	20,000	
Cash		100,000

Withdrawal of a Partner; Bonus to Old Partners

Let us say that Partner C, with a capital balance of $80,000, withdraws, but all partners agree that he takes only $72,000 with him and leaves the remainder in the business.

The entry would be:

Partner C, Capital	80,000	
Cash		72,000
Partner A, Capital		4,000
Partner B, Capital		4,000

Death of a Partner

Partner C dies. His capital account is immediately closed and a liability account is setup for his estate. Let us say that at the time of death Partner C's capital account has a credit balance of $80,000.

The entry would be:

Partner C, Capital	80,000	
C's Estate Payable		80,000

3.2 Legal and Tax Aspects

3.2.1 Legal Aspects

Any change in ownership of a partnership, whether an admission of a new partner, a withdrawal of an old partner or a pooling of interests (adding several new partners at one time) makes an entirely new legal partnership business.

Admission of New Partner

A person admitted as a partner into an existing partnership is liable for all the obligations of the partnership arising before his admission as though he had been a partner when such obligations were incurred, except that his liability shall be satisfied only out of partnership property.

Withdrawal of Old Partner

The dissolution of a partnership does not of itself discharge the existing liability of any partner. The withdrawing partner may be relieved only by entering into an agreement with the creditor.

3.2.2 Tax Aspects

Admission of New Partner

The new partner's tax basis is the sum of

1. the amount of cash contributed
2. the adjusted basis of any noncash assets contributed
3. the share of any partnership liabilities for which he or she is jointly responsible
4. less the old partners' share of any liabilities the new partner contributes to the partnership

Withdrawal of a Partner

A partner withdraws and receives cash from the partnership. The determination of the partner's gain or loss for income-tax purposes is made by comparing (subtracting) the proceeds with his or her tax basis. The *proceeds* are the sum of cash received plus the share of existing partnership liabilities for which he or she is relieved of responsibility.

EXAMPLE

Withdrawing partner has a capital balance of $30,000.

Withdrawing partner is to receive a bonus of $8,000.

The partnership has liabilities of $24,000.

The four partners share profits and losses equally.

The withdrawing partner's tax basis is $29,000.

Computation

Proceeds

Cash distribution ($30,000 capital + $8,000 bonus)	$38,000
Relief of Partnership Liabilities (1/4 of $24,000)	6,000
Total Proceeds	$44,000
Less withdrawing partner's tax basis (given)	– 29,000
Taxable Gain	$15,000

3.3 Federal Income Tax Law and Partnerships

Partnerships report their income to the Internal Revenue Service on Information Tax Returns.

Partnerships pay no federal income tax because each partner is taxed on their share of income on their personal income tax returns.

The tax basis of assets that the partners contribute to the partnership may differ from the accounting basis of these assets.

Illustration

Arnold & Brown form a partnership. Arnold contributes $10,000 in cash, and Brown contributes $2,000 cash and a building with a fair market value of $16,000 subject to a $6,000 mortgage. The mortgage is transferred to the partnership.

General Journal entries:

Cash	10,000	
Arnold, Capital		10,000
Cash	2,000	
Building	16,000	
Mortgage Payable		6,000
Brown, Capital		12,000

Suppose, further, that the tax basis of the building is $11,000, which is $5,000 less than its fair market value of $16,000. So the tax bases of the partners' interests are not equal to the initial balances of their capital accounts.

COMPUTATION OF TAX BASES OF PARTNERS' CAPITAL INTERESTS
Arnold & Brown Partnership
Schedule of Tax Bases of Partners' Capital Interests

Tax Basis of Contributed Assets:	Arnold	Brown
Cash	$10,000	$ 2,000
Building		11,000
Subtotal	$10,000	$13,000
Adjustment to basis for $6,000 mortgage transferred to partnership by Brown and assumed by the partnership	3,000	(3,000)
Tax Bases of Capital Interests	$13,000	$10,000

3.4 Limited Partnership

Rules set up by the Uniform Limited Partnership Act

Limited partners have no obligation for unpaid liabilities of the limited partnership; only general partners have such liability.

Limited partners have no participation in the management of the limited partnership.

Limited partners may invest only cash or other assets in a limited partnership; they may not provide services as their investment.

The last name of a limited partner may not appear in the name of the partnership.

The formation of a limited partnership is evidenced by a *Certificate* filed with the county recorder in the county where the principal office of the partnership is located. It must include:

1. Name and residence of each general partner and limited partner
2. Provision for the return of a limited partner's investment
3. Any priority of one limited partner over other limited partners

4. Any right of limited partners to vote for the election or removal of general partners

5. Termination of the partnership

6. Amendment of the certificate

7. Disposal of all partnership assets

Limited partnerships selling partnerships in *units* must file periodic reports with the Securities and Exchange Commission.

Master Limited Partnerships — Large limited partnerships engaging in ventures such as oil and gas exploration and real estate development, issuing units registered with the Securities and Exchange Commission.

Accounting for Limited Partnerships

1. Limited partners do not have drawing accounts.

2. Limited partnerships should maintain a subsidiary limited partners' ledger.

Income Statements for Limited Partnerships must clearly show the total amount of the net income or loss allocated to the general partners and to the limited partners.

EXAMPLE

BROWN COMPANY (A Limited Partnership) Income Statement For Year Ended December 31, Year 1		
Revenue		$500,000
Cost and Expenses		310,000
Net Income		$190,000
Division of Net Income ($100 per unit based on 1900 weighted-average units outstanding):		
To general partners (30 units)	$3,000	
To limited partners (1870 units)	$187,000	
Total	$190,000	

Statement of Partners' Capital for Limited Partnerships should show the initial investment at the beginning of the year, adding the net income (or deducting the net loss), and deducting any redemption of units, with the final amounts of partners' capital at the end of the year shown. These should be listed in total and per unit for general partners, and also in separate columns for limited partners, and also with separate columns for combined amounts.

EXAMPLE

RANDALL COMPANY
(A Limited Partnership)
Statement of Partners' Capital
For Year Ended December 31, Year 1

	General Partner		Limited Partner		Combined	
	Units	Amount	Units	Amount	Units	Amount
Initial Investment,						
Beginning of Year	30	$30,000	1,870	$1,870,000	1,900	1,900,000
Add: Net Income		3,000		187,000		190,000
Subtotals	30	$33,000	1,870	$2,057,000	1,900	$2,090,000
Less: Redemption						
of Units			−40	−44,000	−40	−$ 44,000
Partners' Capital						
End of Year	30	$33,000	1,830	$2,013,000	1,860	$2,046,000

The Equity Section of the Balance Sheet for a Limited Partnership should distinguish between the amounts assigned to each ownership class.

EXAMPLE

RANDALL COMPANY
(A Limited Partnership)
Balance Sheet
December 31, Year 1

Assets		Liabilities & Partners' Capital		
Current Assets	$ 240,000	Current Liabilities	$100,000	
Other Assets	$2,760,000	Long-term debt	$854,000	
		Total Liabilities		$954,000
		Partners' Capital ($1,100 per unit based on 1,860 units outstanding):		
		General Partners	$ 33,000	
Total Assets	$3,000,000	Limited Partners	$2,013,000	
				$2,046,000
		Total Liabilities and Partners' Capital		$3,000,000

Chapter Three Review Questions

1. When the new partner purchases an old partner's interest in the firm and pays him or her directly, is the amount paid directly listed on the books of the firm?

No. The firm is interested only in the amounts to be debited or credited to the various partners' capital accounts, and these might not be the same amounts as those paid by one partner to another.

2. Is Goodwill considered a tangible asset?

No. Goodwill is intangible because it cannot be touched and thus cannot be readily sold.

3. When a new partner is admitted to the business, are the assets of the firm usually changed to be valued at market value or cost value?

Market value, since a new legal partnership is being formed and assets are often placed on the books at what they could be sold for now.

4. When a partner leaves the business, is his capital account debited or credited?

Debited. Usually a partner's account has a credit balance, and debiting the account for the same amount will close it out.

5. When a partner withdraws from a business, is it possible for him or her to take out more assets than the value of his or her capital balance?

Yes, if all the partners agree to this.

6. When a partner dies, what happens to his or her capital account?

It is closed by debiting the capital account for the amount of the capital balance. A liability account is set up entitled Partner's Estate Payable.

7. Do partnerships, as such, pay a federal income tax?

No, each individual partner reports his or her share of the partnership income on the individual income tax return.

8. Is it possible for the tax basis of assets to differ from the accounting basis of assets?

Yes, because on depreciable assets, such as buildings, the firm may depreciate on a straight-line basis for accounting purposes and on a more rapid depreciation method for tax purposes.

9. Why is it necessary to keep track of tax bases of partners' capital interests?

Because when the partner leaves the business, if the tax basis of the partner's capital interest is less than the proceeds that the partner receives, the difference must be reported on the partner's income tax return as capital gain.

10. Can limited partners vote for the election or removal of general partners?

Only if allowed to do so in the certificate filed with the county recorder.

CHAPTER 4

PARTNERSHIP LIQUIDATION

4.1 Fundamental Procedures

Noncash assets are eventually sold for cash.

Creditors are paid to the extent possible.

The remaining funds, if any, are paid to the partners.

Partners have unlimited liability, so any partner (general partner) may be called upon to contribute additional funds if partnership assets are insufficient to satisfy creditors' claims.

If a partner has a debit balance in his or her capital account, the remaining partners must absorb this debit balance. This gives the remaining partners legal recourse against the partner.

4.1.1 Marshalling of Assets

(Orderly disposal of assets at liquidation according to the Uniform Partnership Act.)

The partners must pay off all partnership debt first. If there are not enough partnership assets to do this, then the debts are paid from the personal assets of the partners, if personal creditors have been paid in full.

After partners' personal debts are paid off, the other liabilities of the partnership can be paid from the partners' credit balances in their capital accounts.

If the personal creditors and the partnership creditors have been paid in full, then a partner's personal assets can be used to pay other partners in order to satisfy the partner's capital deficiency (debit balance).

4.1.2 Protecting the Interests of All Partners

The accountant's job is to protect the interests of all partners.

Accounting records serve as the basis of allocating available assets to creditors and to individual partners.

Each partner will have a keen interest in monitoring the progress of the partnership liquidation.

4.2 Lump-Sum Liquidations

The partnership's assets are gradually sold off for cash.

This cash is then used to pay off the liabilities. Then if there is any money still remaining, the partners are paid in one lump sum.

4.3 Installment Liquidation

Distributions are made to some or all the partners as cash becomes available. In order to be fair to all partners, the accountant should prepare a Schedule of Safe Payments to determine how much, if any, can be paid to which partners at that particular time. (See example on page 27.)

4.4 Cash Distribution Plans

Following is the final cash distribution plan for the partnership of Amos and Benson:

The assets are sold, and losses on the sale of assets are distributed between the partners according to the profit-and-loss ratio — in this case, 70% to Amos and 30% to Benson.

Receivables are collected from customers, and losses distributed between partners.

Liabilities to all creditors other than partners are paid off.

Liability to Partner Amos is paid.

Remainder of cash is distributed according to partners' remaining capital balances. (See example on page 28.)

EXAMPLE

Aaron, Brown, and Cameron Partnership
Schedule of Safe Payments
January 31, 19x2

	Possible Losses	Aaron Capital (50%)	Brown Capital AND Loan (30%)	Cameron Capital (20%)
Partners' equity Jan. 31, 19x2 (Given)		$340,000	$360,000	$160,000
Possible loss on noncash assets (see Statement of Liquidation)	$700,000	($350,000)	($210,000)	($140,000)
Net Subtotal		($ 10,000)	$150,000	$20,000
Possible loss on Contingencies: Cash Withheld	$ 20,000	(10,000)	(6,000)	(4,000)
Net subtotal		(20,000)	144,000	16,000
Possible loss from Aaron (Debit balance allocated 60:40)		$ 20,000	(12,000)	(8,000)
Safe Payments		0	132,000	8,000

As can be seen above, it would be safe, as of January 31, to pay Brown $132,000 and Cameron $8,000.

4.5 Insolvent Partners and Partnerships

According to the Uniform Partnership Act, the order of payment for claims of an insolvent partner in a bankrupt partnership follows:

Pay separate creditors first.

Next pay partnership creditors.

Finally pay fellow partners.

EXAMPLE

AMOS AND BENSON PARTNERSHIP
STATEMENT OF PARTNERSHIP LIQUIDATION
FOR THE PERIOD JANUARY 1, 19x2 TO JANUARY 31, 19x2

	Cash	Noncash Assets	Priority Liabilities	Amos Loan	(70%) Amos Capital	(30%) Benson Capital
Balances, Jan. 1, 19x2	$20,000	$100,000	$40,000	$20,000	$25,000	$35,000
Sale of Inventory	25,000	(30,000)			(3,500)	(1,500)
Subtotal	45,000	70,000			21,500	33,500
Sale of Plant Assets	30,000	(40,000)			(7,000)	(3,000)
Subtotal	75,000	30,000			14,500	30,500
Collection of Receivables	22,000	(30,000)			(5,600)	(2,400)
Subtotal	97,000				8,900	28,100
Payment of Liabilities	(40,000)		(40,000)			
Subtotal	57,000					
Payment of Amos Loan	(20,000)			(20,000)		
Subtotal	37,000					
Final Distribution to Partners	(37,000)				(8,900)	(28,100)

4.6 Dissolution of a Partnership

A dissolution of a partnership is accomplished:

By acts of the partners

1. By the express will of any partner
2. By the withdrawal of any partner
3. By the expulsion of any partner from the business

By operation of law

1. By the death of any partner
2. By the bankruptcy of any partner or the partnership

3. By court decree: insanity of a partner, incapability of a partner to fulfill a contract, partner guilty of misconduct, partner violates contract agreements, whenever the partnership business can be carried on only at a loss.

4.7 Retirement of a Partner

A retiring partner's interest can be purchased by another member of the firm, or the retiring partner can be given cash or other assets.

The retiring partner is not relieved of personal liabilities for partnership debts incurred before retirement, unless creditors agree.

4.8 Incorporating a Partnership

When a partnership incorporates, often some of their assets will be decreased or increased to market value. Let us say we are increasing the value of the inventories by $5,000 and increasing the value of the land by $10,000: (Profits shared equally)

Inventories	5,000	
Land	10,000	
Aaron, Capital		7,500
Brown, Capital		7,500

After this entry, let us say Aaron's capital account is $100,000 and Brown's capital account is $110,000. We now close out the partners' capital accounts and issue corporate common stock, as follows:

Aaron, Capital	100,000	
Brown, Capital	110,000	
Common Stock		210,000

Chapter Four Review Questions

1. What is meant by Unlimited Liability?

When the assets of the partnership are sold, if there isn't enough cash to pay partnership debts, the partners themselves will be forced to pay partnership debts out of their own personal assets.

2. Do limited partners have to pay partnership debts out of their own personal assets?

No. Only general partners may be required to do this.

3. If both the partnership and the partners are in financial trouble, do partners have to pay unpaid partnership debts out of their own personal assets?

Yes, but the partners' personal creditors must be paid in full first.

4. Whose job is it to protect all partners during a partnership liquidation?

It is the accountant's job.

5. In partnership liquidation, are partners paid in one lump sum, or gradually?

Either way the partners or trustee decide.

6. During installment-type liquidation, how does the accountant know how much to distribute to the partners?

By preparing a schedule of safe payments.

7. Let us say that in the past, one of the partners has lent money to the partnership. Who will be paid first, the general creditors or the partner-creditor?

The general creditors.

8. If one partner goes insane, how does this affect the partnership?

It legally ends the partnership.

9. If Partner A sells all his $100,000 interest in the partnership to Partner B for $120,000 which amount is entered on the partnership books?

$100,000.

10. Does Goodwill have a debit or a credit balance?

Debit balance.

CHAPTER 5

ESTATES AND TRUSTS

5.1 Estates and Trusts

Estates and Trusts are similar in their administration and accounting. When a person dies, his or her assets must be gathered together, and either sold or given to heirs according to the will of the deceased, or else according to state law.

5.2 Administering an Estate

The person having custody of the decedent's will deliver it to the probate court. The court issues a letter enabling the executor to proceed with the administration of the estate.

The administrator or executor lists all the decedent's assets and liabilities. Sometimes an appraisor values the assets at the time of death.

The inventory of assets and liabilities and the appraisals are filed with the court.

The fiduciary has authority over all assets of the deceased except the home and exempt property of the surviving spouse and minor children.

The fiduciary collects rents, and pays taxes on the property.

The fiduciary must keep records and render an accounting to the court.

The fiduciary first pays cost and expenses of administration, then reasonable funeral expenses, then allowances to surviving spouse and children of deceased, then debts and taxes, then reasonable medical expenses of deceased's last sickness, then all other debts and taxes according to state law.

5.3 Accounting for Estates

Estates and trusts are accounting entities.

An account, Estate Principle, with a credit balance, is set up to show accountability of the fiduciary. For instance, when cash is received by the fiduciary, the following entry could be made:

Cash—Principal	100,000	
Estate Principal		100,000

When the estate receives a dividend check from a corporation, the following entry would be made:

Cash—Income	3,000	
Estate Income		3,000

When funeral expenses are paid, the following entry could be made:

Funeral Expenses	2,000	
Cash—Principal		2,000

5.4 Estate Principal and Income

The trustee must keep principal cash separate from revenue cash.

5.5 Fiduciary Report

The trustee must report to the court at least once a year. This should include names and addresses of living beneficiaries, trust principal at beginning of the period, dates and sources of acquisitions, gains or losses on investments, deductions from trust principal, and an unpaid claims statement.

5.6 Estate Planning

Prior to death, persons should provide for the orderly transfer of their assets to relatives, charities, and trusts. They should be guided by lawyers and accountants.

Attorneys help in making wills.

Accountants help by minimizing estate taxes and inheritance taxes. Rich or moderately rich people especially need this help.

The Economic Recovery Tax Act of 1981 was set up so that an estimated 99.5% of all estates are no longer subject to Federal Estate Tax. (The estate must total over $600,000 before it is subject to Estate Tax.)

5.7 Fiduciaries

Trustees are people appointed by will or by the court to administer trusts and estates.

An executor is a trustee appointed by the decedent's will.

An administrator is a trustee appointed by the court.

Chapter Five Review Questions

1. *Why are trusts and estates discussed together?*
   Because their accounting is similar.

2. *To whom is the fiduciary responsible?*
   The court.

3. *Who usually pays the funeral expenses?*
   The fiduciary of the estate.

4. *Why does the account, Estate Principal, have a credit balance?*
   Because the fiduciary owes accountability to the estate.

5. *Why is it necessary for the Fiduciary to keep CASH PRINCIPAL separate from CASH INCOME?*
   The law in most states requires this.

6. *How can lawyers help in estate planning?*
   By writing wills for clients.

7. *How can accountants help in estate planning?*
   By advising clients methods of cutting down legally on estate and inheritance taxes.

8. *How much must be the total value of the estate before it is subject to federal estate tax?*

$600,000.

9. *People appointed by the court to administer estates have what title?*

Administrators.

10. *People appointed by the will itself to administer the will have what title?*

Executors.

CHAPTER 6

BANKRUPTCY

6.1 Bankruptcy

Equity Insolvency — Not being able to pay debts as they come due.

Bankruptcy Insolvency — Liabilities exceed Assets.

6.2 Corporate Liquidations, Reorganization, and Restructuring

The following are some methods used by corporations that cannot pay their bills to overcome insolvency:

Raise additional capital by borrowing from banks

Sell more stocks and bonds

Dispose of profitable segments

Combine with another business

Restructure its debts outside of bankruptcy courts

Reorganize through bankruptcy courts

Liquidate

6.3 Bankruptcy Reform Act of 1978

Prologue

1. In earlier times, people who could not pay their debts were thrown into debtors' prisons.

2. The U.S. Constitution gives the federal government control over bankruptcy.

3. Bankruptcy laws have been written and rewritten by Congress periodically since 1800.

35

4. The latest bankruptcy law was passed in 1978 and became effective on October 1, 1979.

5. Two purposes of the present bankruptcy law are the following:
   a. Fair distribution of assets to creditors
   b. Discharge of an honest debtor from debt

6. *Voluntary Bankruptcy*—When a company becomes insolvent it can petition the federal court to begin bankruptcy proceedings. The company lists all assets and liabilities, states when it commenced business, where its records can be found, and when the last property inventory was taken.

7. *Involuntary Bankruptcy*—Creditors of an insolvent company (at least three of them) must sign a petition with the court in order to force the company into bankruptcy. The debt must be $5,000 or greater.

8. The bankruptcy judge appoints a trustee approved by the Office of U.S. Trustee.

The company must surrender all property and books to trustee.

The company must appear at court hearings as required.

Chapter 11 Bankruptcy rules have been broadened by a recent Supreme Court decision, in which individual business people (as well as corporations) can now file for bankruptcy under Chapter 11 and continue operating their business without forced sale.

1. Creditors must agree to a reorganization plan.

2. The reorganization plan is complex and costly.

3. Chapter 11 Bankruptcy is mainly for businesses with debts *over $100,000.*

4. Chapter 13 allows bankruptcy with continued operating privileges for businesses with debts *up to $100,000.*

6.4 Liquidation (Chapter 7 Bankruptcy)

An interim trustee is appointed by the court, or a trustee is elected by the creditors.

Duties of the Trustee

1. Takes control of any assets and sells them for cash.

36

2. Investigates the financial affairs of the debtor.
3. Provides information about the debtor's estate to parties of interest.
4. Examines creditor claims and objects to claims that seem improper.
5. If authorized, operates debtor's business and provides reports of operations and statements of receipts and disbursements.
6. To void transfers of property from debtor to outsiders if this transfer is made to hinder the progress of the fair liquidation.

Order of Liquidation

1. Secured claims are paid first.
2. Unsecured claims are paid in the following order:
   Administrative expenses, trustee fees, legal and accounting fees.
3. Claims incurred between the date of bankruptcy filing and the date when the trustee was appointed.
4. Claims from employees for wages, salaries, and commissions earned within 90 days of filing the petition and not exceeding $2,000 per individual.
5. Claims for contributions to employee benefit plans.
6. Claims of individuals not to exceed $900 from purchase, lease, or rental of property not delivered or services not provided.
7. Claims of governmental units for taxes.
8. Unsecured nonpriority claims.
9. Stockholder claims.

6.5 Reorganization (Chapter 11 Bankruptcy)

In this case, a debtor company may survive insolvency and continue operations if a proposal for reorganization is accepted by the parties involved.

Creditors agree to absorb a partial loss rather than force the company to liquidate.

Creditors and court must be convinced that a greater return will be achieved by helping to rehabilitate the debtor.

Reorganization Plan

1. Must be fair and equitable to all parties.

The debtor corporation files a reorganization plan within the first 120 days after the court order for relief is granted.

Later, the trustee, the creditors' committees, or other interested parties may file reorganization plans.

Examples of some parts of reorganization plans are: merger with other companies, sale of preferred stock, modification of a lien, extension of maturity dates.

After the necessary approval by creditors has been obtained, the court holds a confirmation hearing to confirm that the plan is fair and equitable.

Confirmation by the court discharges the debtor except for claims provided for in the reorganization plan.

This usually involves revaluing the firm's assets and restructuring the liability and capital accounts of the firm. Some creditor classes may become stockholders. Deficit retained earnings balances are eliminated by charges against additional paid-in capital. Similar adjustments apply to quasi-reorganizations that are approved by stockholders, but without the legal formalities of a Chapter 11 reorganization.

6.6 Statement of Affairs

A Statement of Affairs is designed to disclose all the debtor's assets and liabilities according to the classifications that are relevant to liquidation.

Assets

1. Pledged with fully secured creditors
2. Pledged with partially secured creditors
3. Free assets

Liabilities

1. Liabilities with priority
2. Fully secured creditors
3. Partially secured creditors
4. Unsecured creditors

Other considerations

1. Assets are listed at net realizable value

6.7 Role of the Trustee

The trustee is the central figure in any liquidation. The trustee:

1. Recovers all property belonging to the insolvent company.
2. Preserves the estate from further deterioration.
3. Sells noncash assets.
4. Makes distributions to the proper claimants.
5. May have to continue operating the company.
6. May appoint outside attorneys, accountants, and consultants.
7. May also void any transfer of assets made by the debtor within 90 days prior to filing for bankruptcy.
8. Must make reports to court and other interested parties.

The trustee should make a Statement of Receipt and Liquidation:

1. Give the amount of the account balances on the date the order for relief was filed by the bankrupt.
2. Give the cash receipts generated by the sale of the debtor's property.
3. Give the cash disbursements made by the trustee to wind up the affairs of the business and to pay secured creditors.
4. Give information regarding the write-off of assets and the recognition of unrecorded liabilities.

Chapter Six Review Questions

1. What is the term for a firm's inability to pay its debts as they become due?

Equity insolvency.

2. Is it possible for an insolvent company to restructure its debts without going through a bankruptcy court?

Sometimes it can be done, especially if the creditors are cooperative.

3. If a debtor goes through bankruptcy court proceedings, is he or she free of debt?

Yes.

4. *If at least three creditors petition the court to force a company into bankruptcy, what is this called?*

Involuntary bankruptcy.

5. *How is a Trustee in bankruptcy chosen?*

The temporary trustee is chosen by the Court; a permanent trustee can be chosen by the creditors.

6. *What is the difference between "Chapter 7 Bankruptcy" and "Chapter 11 Bankruptcy"?*

Chapter 7 Bankruptcy is liquidation where all the company assets are sold and the company disbanded. On the other hand, Chapter 11 Bankruptcy is a form of reorganization where the insolvent company is allowed to continue in business.

7. *What are Quasi-Reorganizations?*

Semi-reorganizations agreed to by debtor and creditors without going through bankruptcy court. This often includes bondholders becoming stockholders, and deficit retained earnings balances being eliminated by charges against additional paid-in capital.

8. *What is Troubled-Debt Restructuring?*

Revising the corporation without going through quasi-reorganization and without going through bankruptcy court. This often consists of the creditors relieving the debtor of some of the debt, reducing interest rates, extending debt maturities.

9. *What is a Statement of Affairs?*

A financial statement listing debtor's assets and liabilities at the time of liquidation.

10. *What is the main job of the Securities and Exchange Commission?*

To see that investors and potential investors have reliable information concerning corporations that trade stock publicly.

CHAPTER 7

GOVERNMENT REGULATION OF ACCOUNTING AND REPORTING

7.1 Government Regulation

Government agencies regulate many aspects of accounting work, and some agencies require reports from accountants. The main such agencies are: Securities and Exchange Commission, Federal Communications Commission, Interstate Commerce Commission, Department of Transportation. Non-governmental agencies doing some regulation of accountants are: the stock exchanges and National Association of Securities Dealers.

7.2 Securities and Exchange Commission (SEC)

The SEC was set up in 1934 to regulate the securities market in the United States.

The three main interests of the Securities and Exchange Commission are:

1. Full and fair disclosure of all material facts concerning securities offered for public investment.
2. Initiating litigation of fraud cases when detected.
3. Providing for the registration of securities offered for public investment.

The set up of Securities and Exchange Commission is:

1. Five commissioners appointed by U.S. President with approval of U.S. Senate.
2. Main office is in Washington, D.C., but there are regional and branch offices in most major financial centers in the U.S.

41

The chief powers of the Securities and Exchange Commission are:

1. To require firms issuing new securities to supply the Securities and Exchange Commission and the public with registration information and prospectuses.

2. To require securities exchanges, securities dealers, and over-the-counter stock dealers to register with the Securities and Exchange Commission.

3. To regulate public utilities.

4. To regulate the issuance of debt securities and trust indentures.

5. To regulate the activities of investment companies.

6. To regulate the activities of financial advisors.

SEC Regulation S-X — Form and Content of Financial Statements — This regulation shows accountants how to prepare reports for the SEC.

Accounting Series Releases — Up-to-date information for preparing reports for the SEC, issued by the SEC.

Form 10-K — Annual reports of corporations filed with the SEC within 90 days after the end of the current fiscal year to provide for continuing disclosure of important company facts and financial statements.

Form 8-K — Current reports filed by corporations within 15 days after the occurrence of a reportable event that prudent investors should know about, such as changes in the control of the company, buying or selling of assets, bankruptcy, changes in the company's certifying accountant.

The impact of the SEC on accounting is:

1. Corporations now usually integrate reports to shareholders with reports to the SEC, so they both get the same or similar reports.

2. The SEC allows the private sector (Financial Accounting Standards Board and the American Institute of Certified Public Accountants) the first opportunity to resolve accounting issues. If Financial Accounting Standards Board fails to act in a reasonable time, the SEC will exercise its own authority.

7.3 Federal Trade Commission (FTC)

The FTC was set up to enforce the Clayton Anti-Trust Act. It helps prevent unfair methods of competition in commerce and unfair or deceptive acts or practices in commerce.

The Federal Trade Commission can issue "Cease and Desist Orders" against violators. It works closely with the U.S. Department of Justice.

A company with assets or sales of at least $10 million that plans to acquire a manufacturing company with assets or sales of at least $10 million must file a detailed 21-page form 30 days before the planned date of consummation. The FTC can, if it wishes, file preliminary court injunctions to block the proposed combinations.

EXAMPLE

In 1986 the FTC sought injunction against the proposed sale by Philip Morris Co. of Seven-Up Co., its subsidiary, to PepsiCo. Inc., and against the proposed purchase of Dr. Pepper Co. by Coca-Cola Co., because the transactions would give Coke and Pepsi nearly 80% of the soft drink market in the U.S. Shortly thereafter, Philip Morris announced it would seek another buyer.

7.4 Federal Communications Commission (FCC)

The FCC's responsibilities include:

It has broad authority over all interstate communications by wire, radio, television.

It conducts investigations, grants licenses, assigns broadcasting frequencies.

It requires reports from interstate common carriers.

FCC reports include information about the corporation's stocks, dividends, debts, property values, number of employees, salaries, net income or losses.

FCC develops policies regarding corporations' rates, services, accounting, reporting.

FCC conducts research projects, prescribes depreciation rates, and develops and enforces accounting rules for carriers.

7.5 Interstate Commerce Commission

The ICC's (set up by ICC Act of 1887) responsibilities include:

It regulates common carriers that cross state lines.

It regulates railroads, ships, pipeline companies, motor carriers.

It sets up uniform systems of accounts.

It requires reports concerning stock, dividends, stockholders, retained earnings, number of employees, net income or loss.

It attempts to work with Financial Accounting Standards Board in setting up a uniform system of accounts.

7.6 Department of Transportation

The Department of Transportation's responsibilites include:

It regulates public transportation services.

It requires reports from air carriers.

It sets up uniform accounting systems for all public transportation services receiving federal grants.

It requires reports yearly from public transportation systems which must be audited by CPAs.

It sets up uniform accounting methods so carriers can file proper reports.

It requires information about corporate officers, directors, financial statements, accounting methods, depreciation methods, pension plans.

7.7 Stock Exchanges

The New York Stock Exchange and American Stock Exchange require corporations listed on these exchanges to:

Make public disclosure of important developments in the corporation.

Publish annual report to stockholders.

Make information available in annual report on stock options and on treasury stock.

Publish quarterly statements on sales and earnings.

Notify the exchange of substantial charges against retained earnings or other capital accounts.

Notify the exchange regarding substantial changes in accounting methods.

Notify the exchange when the company changes its independent public accounting firm.

Chapter Seven Review Questions

1. What bureau provides for the registration of securities offered for public investment?

Securities and Exchange Commission.

2. What are the names of the main reports required from corporations by the Securities and Exchange Commission?

Yearly reports, called 10-K, and occasional reports, called 8-K.

3. Why does the Securities and Exchange Commission issue Accounting Series Releases?

To keep readers up to date with changes in rules for preparing reports to the Securities and Exchange Commission.

4. Does the Securities and Exchange Commission try to make accounting rules and regulations?

Usually it allows the private sector (Financial Accounting Standards Board and American Institute of Certified Public Accountants) a chance to make these decisions before it steps in.

5. What happens when a company does not follow a Cease and Desist Order issued by the Federal Trade Commission?

The Federal Trade Commission asks the U.S. Department of Justice to take the case to court. The FTC can also take the case to court.

6. What governmental agency assigns radio broadcast frequencies?

The Federal Communications Commission.

7. *What governmental department requires accounting reports from airlines?*

Department of Transportation.

8. *Is there a governmental agency that tries to set up uniform accounting systems for railroads?*

Yes, the Interstate Commerce Commission.

9. *How can a non-governmental firm, like the stock exchanges, make accounting rules?*

By requiring firms wanting to be listed on the stock exchange to follow these rules.

CHAPTER 8

GOVERNMENT REGULATION OF INDUSTRY

8.1 Governmental Regulation of Certain Industries

Although most industries are not directly regulated by the government, a few are. Some of them follow:

8.2 Franchising

Franchising is a system whereby one company grants business rights to another through a contract to operate a franchised business for a specified period of time. (Example: McDonald's)

Franchisor — The company granting the business rights.

Franchisee — The company receiving the business rights.

1. The Franchise Itself: the franchisor generally provides a variety of services and products to the franchisee in exchange for fees and charges for products.

2. Franchisor often provides: trademark, reputation, products, procedures, manpower, equipment, perhaps some operating capital.

3. Franchisee often provides: capital, managerial and operating resources.

4. Benefits of franchising to franchisor: wide distribution of franchisor's product or service without having to provide all the capital or the day-to-day management.

5. Benefits of franchising to franchisee: can establish a business with a known reputation, with less capital, with managerial assistance available, with less likelihood of failure.

6. The initial franchising fee is debited as an intangible asset on the books of the franchisee and written off over the life of the franchise. Let us assume the franchisee pays the franchisor $19,000.

Franchise	19,000	
Cash		19,000

If the franchise is for five years, $^1/_5$ of the $19,000 franchise fee could be written off at the end of the first year:

Franchise Expense	3,800	
Franchise		3,800

8.3 Real Estate

The industry has a high ratio of borrowed capital to equity capital. This, along with the fluctuating cost of money, is the cause of the industry's susceptibility to extreme economic cycles. It is often difficult or time-consuming to turn land investments into money when needed.

1. Profit should not be recognized (put down on books) until the sale actually has occurred.

2. Example: Let us say that a house and lot with a cost basis of $20,000 was sold for cash of $25,000. The following would be entered on the seller's books:

Cash	25,000	
Real Estate		20,000
Gain on Sale		5,000

3. *Installment Method of recording investment income* — Each receipt of cash from the buyer includes a return of cost and a realization of profit.

EXAMPLE

Assume that our company sold a house and lot for $80,000. The terms of the sale called for a cash down payment of $3,000, with a mortgage note bearing interest at 10% for the balance. The note is for 30 years, with an annual payment (principal and interest) of $8,274. The property had a cost to us of $50,000. We use the Installment Method.

February 1	Cash		3,000	
	Receivable from Realty Sale		77,000	
	Installment Sale			80,000
	To record the sale			
1	Cost of Installment Sale		50,000	
	Inventory of Real Estate			50,000
28	Installment Sale		80,000	
	Cost of Installment Sale			50,000
	Deferred Gross Profits on Inst. Sale			30,000
	To record deferred profit on installment sales made during Feb.			
28	Deferred Gross Profit on Installment Sales		1,125	
	Realized Gross Profit on Inst. Sales			1,125
	To record realized profit on inst. sales computed as follows: $3,000 × ($30,000 gross profit/ $80,000 selling price, or 37.5%)			
Following Year				
January 31	Cash		8,274	
	Interest Revenue			7,700
	Receivable from Sale			574
	To record annual payment (Interest 10% × $77,000 = $7,700)			
31	Deferred Gross Profit on Installment Sales		215	
	Realized Gross Profit on Installment Sales			215
	To record realized profit on inst. sales computed as follows: $574 × ($30,000 gross profit/ $80,000 selling price, or 37.5%)			

8.4 Banking

Banking is regulated at both federal and state levels.

National Banks have national charters and are regulated by the office of the Controller of the Currency. Must belong to Federal Reserve System. Must have deposits insured by Federal Deposit Insurance Corporation.

State Banks have state charters, are supervised by state governments, and may join FDIC.

Trends

Bank accounting is becoming more like generally accepted accounting principles used in other areas of business.

Bank Accounting

1. Banks balance their books daily and have a daily statement of financial condition.
2. Banks cannot usually own stock in other firms. Often 25% to 30% of their assets are invested in government bonds or in high-grade industrial bonds.
3. Often about 55% of total assets are in loans.
4. Customer deposits are the major liabilities of banks.
5. Capital Surplus in a bank statement is similar to a combination of Paid-In Capital and Retained Earnings in other businesses.
6. Banks do not separate assets and liabilities into long- and short-term.
7. The Securities and Exchange Commission has great control of bank accounting.

8.5 Insurance

Life Insurance started around 1700 in England. It is a method of spreading risks among many persons exposed to similar hazards.

Other forms of insurance existed long before 1700. Today, types of insurance include the following: fire, marine, commercial, home owner's, accident and health, workmen's compensation, auto liability and physical damage, fidelity and surety, glass, burglary and theft, boiler and machinery.

The organization of insurance companies can be broken down into the following:

1. *Stock Company* — Owned and controlled by stockholders.

2. *Mutual Company* — Owned and controlled by existing policy-holders.

Use of premium money — To pay for all losses, cover expenses, and make a small profit.

Reinsurance — Large policies resold to other insurance companies.

Regulation — Usually by state governments through their insurance departments. States require fair dealing between insurance companies and policyholders and uniform financial reporting, and try to promote insurance company solvency.

1. States usually require standard provisions in insurance policies.

2. States license insurance salesmen.

3. States require insurance companies to file detailed annual reports.

4. Since 1972, insurance company reports have grown closer to generally accepted accounting principles.

5. Premium income should be recognized when received over the life of the insurance contract.

6. Expenses should be recorded when incurred.

8.6 Public Utilities

Public Utilities are natural monopolies with great amounts of capital investment. Utilities include electric companies, natural gas, telephone, and water companies.

These firms are regulated by the state government.

Regulatory agencies on the national level:

1. Federal Energy Regulatory Commission (electricity, gas, oil) (formerly the Federal Power Commission), part of the Dept. of Energy

2. Atomic Energy Commission (nuclear fuel)

3. Federal Communications Commission (telephone)

4. Securities and Exchange Commission (public utilities)

Many public utilities are regulated by both federal and state governments.

Items regulated

1. Designates of operating areas for the utility
2. Set rates to be charged
3. Set up accounting policies and a uniform chart of accounts
4. Process customer complaints
5. Set up utility operating methods

Most utilities today keep books according to generally accepted accounting principles.

Utility plants usually function at cost. When new facilities are being built, an asset account entitled *Construction Work in Progress* can be debited and an offset account Allowance for Funds Used during Construction is credited for construction costs, for interest on borrowed funds, and for dividends on preferred stock, as follows:

Construction Work in Progress	10,000	
Allowance for Funds Used during Construction		10,000

Interest on borrowed funds, dividends on preferred stock, and costs associated with common stock equity are commonly capitalized during the construction of a new facility. Because interest during construction is capitalized to an asset account (Construction Work in Progress being debited in the entry just above), the offset or credit is to a revenue account generally called Allowance for Funds Used during Construction. In preparing an income statement, the credit arising from borrowed funds should be deducted from interest expense; that arising from other funds (common and preferred stock) is included as other income. In addition to the interest, direct and overhead costs and general expenses applicable to the construction are also capitalized. Construction costs are important for both control and rate-making purposes, so extensive accounting and reporting systems exist for the construction activity.

Inventories of fossil fuel, such as coal, are current assets.

Nuclear fuel is a quasi-fixed asset because of its longer life.

1. Nuclear fuel produces additional fuel.
2. Nuclear fuel has an added by-product — plutonium.
3. For the above reasons, there may be a negative salvage value.

Income Tax Accounting vs. Generally Accepted Accounting Principles for utilities

1. Straight-line depreciation for generally accepted accounting principles, and faster methods for tax purposes. (These faster methods might be sum-of-years-digits method or double-declining-balance method of depreciation.)
2. Interest and construction overhead should be capitalized for generally accepted accounting principles but expensed for tax purposes.

Reporting of utilities to the Securities and Exchange Commission

1. SEC requires the calculation of earnings coverage for five years. (Earnings coverage is the ratio of earnings to fixed charges plus preferred dividends. Preferred dividends are here treated much like fixed charges.)
2. Allowance for Funds Used during Construction is used in computing earnings.

Chapter Eight Review Questions

1. Why is the contracting business so risky?

If the contractor bids low and gets the bid, he or she may lose money. Expenses will probably be greater than contract income. On the other hand, if the contractor bids high, he or she loses the bid.

2. If contracting is so risky, how can contractors stay in business?

By good business management, good accounting, and making proper business decisions.

3. In the construction industry, how does Fixed-Price Accounting differ from Cost-Plus Accounting?

In Fixed-Price Accounting, the total income for the job is stated in the contract. This is the amount that will be received, no matter what the costs are.

In Cost-Plus Accounting, the amount that the contractor will receive will be the total of the costs of the job plus an agreed-on profit.

4. *What is the Completed-Contract Method of Accounting?*

The revenue is not put down on the books until the job is done.

5. *What type of account is Construction in Progress?*

Asset.

6. *What is the Percentage-of-Completion Method of accounting?*

This method allows contractors to record a certain percentage of income at year's end, even though the project is not completed.

7. *Why is franchising important?*

In today's economy, many large firms sign franchise agreements, allowing franchisees to carry on business under the trade name of the franchisor. (Example: Kentucky Fried Chicken)

8. *Who is the Franchisor?*

The company that grants the business rights (The Central Headquarters of the Kentucky Fried Chicken Company).

9. *Who is the Franchisee?*

The company that receives the rights to use the Kentucky Fried Chicken name.

10. *In most of the franchise contracts, who provides most of the day-to-day management?*

The franchisee.

CHAPTER 9

STATE AND LOCAL GOVERNMENTAL ACCOUNTING

9.1 Accounting Standards for State and Local Governments

Governmental Accounting Standards Board — A private organization under the Financial Accounting Foundation — is the chief standard-setter for state and local government accounting.

Established in 1984, the Governmental Accounting Standards Board has issued statements regarding deferred compensation plans, deposits with financial institutions, and accounting for employee pensions.

9.2 General Fund

The General Fund records all financial resources that are not accounted for in another fund.

A fund is a segregated collection of both asset and equity accounts, together with related revenue and expenditure accounts that describe a particular aspect of the organization.

The General Fund is usually the largest of the governmental funds.

Other funds might include: capital projects fund, debt service fund, utility fund, scholarship trust fund, etc.

Modified Accrual Method of Accounting — Property taxes are accrued by the government when levied, but all other revenues are recognized when the related cash is collected. All expenditures for supplies require a purchase order, which is recorded as an encumbrance.

EXAMPLE

CITY GOVERNMENT BOOKS

Jan. 1, 19x6: Taxes Receivable—Current	270,000	
Revenues Control—Property taxes		258,000
Allowance for Uncollectible		
Taxes—Current		12,000
(Property taxes of $270,000 are		
levied, including $12,000 estimated		
uncollectible)		
Jan. 20, 19x6: Cash	2,000	
Taxes Receivable—Delinquent		2,000
(Back tax monies of $2,000		
are received)		
Jan. 20, 19x6: Allowance for Uncollectible Taxes,		
Delinquent	300	
Taxes Receivable—Delinquent		300
(To write off delinquent taxes		
deemed uncollectible)		
Jan. 20, 19x6: Cash	50,000	
Notes Payable		50,000
(City Government borrows money from		
the bank giving the bank a note)		
July 15, 19x6: Notes Payable	50,000	
Interest Expense	250	
Cash		50,250
(City Government pays the bank		
the principal plus interest)		
July 31, 19x6: Cash	260,000	
Taxes Receivable—Current		260,000
(Some of the taxes are collected		
by the City Government)		

Recording Encumbrances—An encumbrance is recorded when a purchase order is approved by the city:

Jan. 15, 19x7 Encumbrances Control	176,250	
Fund Balance Reserved for		
Encumbrances		176,250
(Encumbrances for supplies recorded)		

During 19x7 vouchers totaling $176,000 (these had been encumbered for $176,250) were approved for payment as follows:

Dec. 31, 19x7 Fund Balance Reserved for		
Encumbrances	176,250	
Encumbrances Control		176,250
(To reverse the preceding		
entry for encumbrances)		
Dec. 31, 19x7 Expenditures Control	176,000	
Vouchers Payable		176,000
(Payment of vouchers is authorized		
by the proper administrator)		
Dec. 31, 19x7 Vouchers Payable	176,000	
Cash		176,000
(This entry is made when the checks		
are actually written and mailed)		

9.3 Interfund Transactions

Let us say that the City owns the electrical utility. During the month the City uses $50,000 worth of electricity.

GENERAL FUND TRANSACTION

Jan. 31, 19x5 Expenditure—Electricity	50,000	
Cash		50,000

ENTERPRISE FUND—CITY-OWNED UTILITY

| Jan. 31, 19x5 | Cash | 50,000 | |
| | Revenue | | 50,000 |

Interfund Loans — Let us say that the General Fund makes a long-term loan to an enterprise fund (such as a city-owned public utility).

GENERAL FUND TRANSACTION

Jan. 31, 19x5	Advances to Enterprise Fund	10,000	
	Cash		10,000
	(General Fund loans $10,000 to Enterprise Fund. The account, Advances to Enterprise Fund, is an asset)		

Because such an advance represents an asset to the General Fund that is not spendable, a fund balance reserve must also be recorded, as follows:

Jan. 31, 19x5	Unreserved Fund Balance	10,000	
	Fund Balance Reserved for Advances to Enterprise Fund		10,000
	($10,000 is taken out of the Unreserved Fund Balance and placed in the Reserved)		

ENTERPRISE FUND TRANSACTION

Jan. 31, 19x5	Cash	10,000	
	Advances from General Fund		10,000
	(Advances is a liability account)		
	(Money received by Enterprise Fund from General Fund)		

Accounting for Federal Grants to the City on the City Books. Let us say the federal government is giving the City $150,000 for a new fire truck. At the time the cash is received or the federal grant is approved, the following entry is made:

March 31, 19x5	Cash (or) Grants Receivable	150,000	
	Deferred Revenue		150,000
	(Deferred Revenue is a		
	liability account)		

When the voucher is made out to pay for the fire truck, the following entry is made:

Expenditures Control—Equipment	150,000	
Vouchers Payable		150,000

When the check is written to pay for the fire truck, the following entry is made:

Vouchers Payable	150,000	
Cash		150,000

At the same time, an entry is made to close out the liability account, Deferred Revenue, and to credit the revenue account, as follows:

Deferred Revenue	150,000	
Revenues Control—Federal Grants		150,000

9.4 Capital Fund Projects

Capital Fund projects occur when financial resources are set aside for the acquisition or construction of major fixed assets such as a library or a civic center. Sources for capital projects funds might be: long-term debt, transfers from the general fund, and grants from state and federal governments.

EXAMPLE

The City sells $100,000 bonds to finance a library at a premium of $7,000.

April 30, 19x5 Cash	107,000	
Bonds Payable (or Other		
Financing Sources Control)		100,000
Premium on Bonds		7,000

Premium of $7,000 is transferred to Debt Service Fund.

April 30, 19x5 Premium on Bonds	7,000	
Cash		7,000

A state grant for the library in the amount of $10,000 is announced. $3,000 is received now, and the other $7,000 is promised for later.

May 31, 19x5 Cash	3,000	
Due from State Government	7,000	
Revenues Control—inter-		
governmental—state grant		10,000

A contract was entered into with Brown Construction Company to build a major part of the library building for $80,000. The $80,000 encumbrance is recorded as follows:

June 15, 19x5 Encumbrances Control	80,000	
Fund Balance Reserved for		
Encumbrances		80,000

During the year, expenditures on the building came to $40,000 of which $35,000 was paid in cash and the other $5,000 owed.

Dec. 31, 19x5 Fund Balance Reserve for Encumbrances	40,000	
Encumbrances Control		40,000
(To remove the $40,000		
from being encumbered)		

Dec. 31, 19x5	Expenditures Control	40,000	
	Contracts Payable		35,000
	Contracts Payable—Retained Percentage		5,000
	(To record the year's expenditure)		
Dec. 31, 19x5	Contracts Payable	35,000	
	Cash		35,000
	(To record the first-year payment to the contractor)		

9.5 Debt Service Funds

Debt Service Funds are similar to sinking funds. They are required where legally or contractually mandated, or when resources are being accumulated for future maturities of debt, such as with bonds and interest.

CITY BOOKS
DEBT SERVICE FUND

Jan. 1, 19x6	Due from General Fund	5,000	
	Other Financing Sources Control		5,000
	(To show that General Fund owes Debt Service Fund $5,000 as of the first of the year for debt service)		
Jan. 1, 19x6	Cash	5,000	
	Due from General Fund		5,000
	(To show the actual cash transaction from General Fund to Debt Service Fund)		
Jan. 2, 19x6	Investments	5,000	
	Cash		5,000
	(Debt Service Fund administrator invests the money. Investments is a long-term asset account.)		

Several years later, the Debt Service Fund manager sells investments which cost $5,000 for $5,500. Of this, $200 was interest that had accrued and the other $300 was interest actually earned this year.

Dec. 31, 1990 Cash	5,500	
Investments		5,000
Interest Receivable		200
Revenues Control—Interest		300

The manager reinvests part of the money in other investments:

Dec. 31, 1990 Investments	3,000	
Cash		3,000

One year later, an entry is made to record interest earned but not yet collected:

Dec. 31, 1991 Interest Receivable	300	
Revenues Control—Interest		300

Bond interest coupons are paid on March 31.

March 31, 1991 Expenditures Control—Interest	500	
Cash		500

9.6 Fixed Assets

Fixed assets are maintained on a cost basis except that donated assets are recorded at their fair value at the time of receipt of gift. Few governmental units ever record depreciation on general fixed assets.

Fixed assets for governments are usually classified into Land, Buildings, Improvements other than Buildings, Equipment, and Construction in Progress. Equity in general fixed assets should be identified with the source of monies from which the general fixed assets are acquired. That is, an equity account should be maintained for each fund that provides general fixed assets.

9.7 Long-Term Debt

General long-term liabilities are not secured by the general fixed assets but are secured by the general credit rating and revenue-raising powers of the governmental unit.

Recording the Issuance of Long-Term Debt should be recorded at face value, not at the amount of cash received. Let us say that $100,000 bonds were sold for $103,000.

CITY OF EVANSVILLE

Amount to be Provided for		
Retirement of Term Bonds	100,000	
Term Bonds Payable		100,000

9.8 The Nature of Fund Accounting

A fund is a fiscal and accounting entity with a self-balancing set of accounts recording cash and other financial resources together with all related liabilities and residual equities or balances and changes therein, which are segregated for the purpose of carrying on specific activities or attaining certain objectives in accordance with special regulation, restrictions, or limitations.

The familiar debit and credit framework holds for the recording of transactions and events in the accounting systems of each fund.

The self-balancing feature is not adequate by itself.

There is a need for both a general long-term debt account group and a general fixed assets account group.

1. Each of these account groups has a self-balancing set of accounts and equal debits and credits.

2. These account groups are not funds because they are not fiscal entities that have transactions.

9.9 Types of Funds

The National Council on Government Accounting specifies eight types of funds that should be used by state and local governments. These funds are classified as Governmental Funds, Proprietary Funds, and Fiduciary Funds as follows:

63

9.9.1 Governmental Funds

The General Fund — to account for all financial resources except those required to be accounted for in another fund.

Special Revenue Funds — to account for the proceeds of specific revenue sources that are legally restricted to expenditure for specified purposes.

Capital Projects Funds — to account for financial resources to be used for the acquisition or construction of major capital facilities other than those financed by proprietary funds, special assessment funds, and trust funds.

Debt Service Funds — to account for the accumulation of resources for, and the payment of, general long-term debt principal and interest.

Special Assessment Funds — to account for the financing of public improvements or services deemed to benefit the properties against which special assessments are levied.

9.9.2 Proprietary Funds

Enterprise Funds — to account for operations

1. that are financed and operated in a manner similar to private business enterprises — where the intent of the governing body is that the costs (expenses, including depreciation) of providing goods or services to the general public on a continuing basis be financed or recovered primarily through user charges, or

2. where the governing body has decided that periodic determination of revenues earned, expenses incurred, and/or net income is appropriate for capital maintenance, public policy, management control, accountability, or other purposes.

Internal Service Funds — to account for the financing of goods or services provided by one department or agency to other departments or agencies of the governmental unit, or to other governmental units, on a cost-reimbursement basis.

9.9.3 Fiduciary Funds

Trust and Agency Funds — to account for assets held by a governmental unit in a trustee capacity or as an agent for individuals, private organizations, other governmental units, and/or other funds. These include

1. Expendable Trust Funds
2. Nonexpendable Trust Funds
3. Pension Trust Funds
4. Agency Funds

9.10 Budgetary Entries

On January 1, 19x1 when the budget of the City is approved, a general journal entry is made to record the budget in the accounts of the General Fund. The entry is:

Estimated Revenues	400,000	
Appropriations		395,000
Fund Balance		5,000
To record the budget for the year		
1/1/19x1 to 12/31/19x2		

Under the modified accrual basis of accounting, revenues are recognized (recorded on the books) in the period in which they become available and are measurable. Revenue from property taxes is recognized when taxpayers are billed, and revenues from garbage collection and other city services is recognized when bills are rendered for services performed. But revenue from sales taxes, licenses, permits, fines, and the like cannot be measured objectively until cash is actually received. If taxes are collected in a period before they become available to finance expenditures, the amount received is recorded as a liability (deferred taxes), and it is not put down on the books as revenue until the succeeding period when it becomes available to cover expenditures.

When the treasurer of the City sends out property tax bills, revenue is recognized as follows:

Taxes Receivable—Current	300,000	
Estimated Uncollectible Taxes—Current		2,000
Revenue		298,000
To record the property tax levy		

(This entry assumes that .67% of property tax levies will not be collectible. Therefore, revenue is only recognized for 99.33% of the amount billed. Uncollectible taxes are not expenses in governmental accounting, but are revenue adjustments.

Collections of property taxes are recorded in the usual manner for receivables as follows:

Cash	190,000	
Taxes Receivable—Current		190,000
To record collection of current property taxes		

When bills for the city-owned water utility are sent out, the entry is recorded:

Accounts Receivable	15,000	
Revenue		15,000
To record charges for city water service		

Later collection of the amount billed would be entered on the books as follows:

Cash	15,000	
Accounts Receivable		15,000
To record collection of receivables for water utility service		

Revenue from most other sources is recognized as cash received. Thus, the collection of fees from business licenses is recorded as follows:

Cash	3,000	
Revenue		3,000
To record collection of license fees		

Under modified accrual basis of accounting, expenditures such as salaries, supplies, utilities, and fixed assets are recorded as expenditures *when the related liabilities are incurred.* In each of these cases, the net financial resources (assets minus liabilities) are reduced when the liabili-

66

ties are incurred, because the related resources are not recognized as assets of the general fund.

When salaries are paid or liabilities for salaries are incurred, a General Fund entry is made:

Expenditures	25,000	
Cash		25,000
To record payment of salaries		

When liabilities for salaries are incurred at month's end, but not yet paid, the following entry is made:

Expenditures	3,000	
Salaries Payable		3,000
To record liability for wages incurred		

Supply acquisitions are normally accounted for under the purchase method and are recorded as expenditures when the related liability is incurred.

Expenditures	5,000	
Vouchers Payable		5,000
To record the purchase of operating supplies		

This entry decreases the net assets of the general fund because supply purchases are recorded as expenditures rather than as assets. If $1/5$ the supplies are on hand at the balance sheet date, the supplies on hand would be recorded as follows:

Supplies Inventory	1,000	
Reserve for Supplies Inventory		1,000

This entry recognizes the prepaid asset, Supplies Inventory, while the reserve for supplies is reported in the fund equity section of the balance sheet as a *Reservation of Fund Balance*. This reservation is not available for appropriation, since it is tied up in unappropriable resources.

9.10.1 Encumbrances

It is important to keep expenditures within authorized levels, since expenditures in a period are limited by law to those for which appropriations have been made. Overspending could result when expenditures are approved without considering outstanding purchase orders or unperformed contracts. To prevent this type of situation, encumbrance accounting is used. Encumbrance accounting provides additional control over expenditures. *Encumbrance Means Commitment* in unperformed contracts.

If supplies expected to cost $1,500 are ordered, the following entry is made when the purchase order is placed:

Encumbrances	1,500	
Reserve for Encumbrances		1,500
To record a purchase order for supplies estimated to cost $1,500		

(This information helps prevent overspending because encumbrances can be deducted from Unexpended Appropriations to determine unencumbered appropriations, for example):

Appropriations (authorized expenditures)	$14,000
Less:Expenditures to date	10,000
Unexpended appropriations	4,000
Less:Encumbrances	1,500
Unencumbered appropriations	2,500

When the supplies ordered are received, the entry to record the encumbrance is reversed as follows:

Reserve for Encumbrances	1,500	
Encumbrances		1,500

The actual entry to record the supplies is unaffected by the encumbrance entries and is recorded for the actual amount of the invoice. If the supplies on order actually cost $1,400, the expenditure is recorded as follows:

Expenditures	1,400	
Vouchers Payable		1,400

9.11 Accounting for Proprietary Funds

Proprietary funds are used to account for the financing of goods and services provided by one department or agency to other departments or agencies of the governmental unit, or to other governmental units, on a cost reimbursement basis. Since the objective of these funds is to maintain capital and/or produce income, full accrual accounting procedures are applicable. Thus, these funds have revenue and expense, *Not Expenditure,* accounts.

Centralized purchasing, motor pools, and printing shops are among the more frequent operations accounted for through proprietary funds at the state and local levels.

9.11.1 Accounting to a Proprietary Fund

Assume that the City creates a Central Motor Pool Fund with a cash contribution of $300,000 from the General Fund and a contribution of existing motor vehicles with a fair value of $130,000. The cash contribution is recorded as a $300,000 transfer in the General Fund, and the equipment transferred is removed from the records of the general fixed assets account group at its original cost, or book value if accumulated depreciation has been recorded. In the records of the Central Motor Pool Fund, the following entry is made:

Cash	300,000	
Motor Vehicles	130,000	
Contribution from Municipality		430,000

During the first year of operations, the motor pool supplies motor pool vehicles to municipal departments and bills these departments at a predetermined rate based on miles driven. The rate is set to cover all costs of operating the motor pool and servicing the vehicles, including the cost of replacing worn-out vehicles. Journal entries to record revenue and expense transactions and year-end entries are shown in summary form:

Due from General Fund	70,000	
Due from Special Assessments Fund	20,000	
Due from Enterprise Fund	30,000	
Service Revenue		120,000
To charge user funds for vehicle services		
Cash	100,000	
Due from General Fund		70,000
Due from Enterprise Fund		30,000
To record collections from user funds		

9.11.2 Accounting for Fiduciary Funds

Fiduciary funds are used to account for assets held by a governmental unit as trustee or agent for individuals, private organizations, and other governmental units. This grouping includes both trust funds and agency funds. A separate agency or trust fund is required for each agreement under which the governmental unit acts as agent or trustee.

Assume that Monominee County collects property taxes for its own purposes as well as for the towns of Crestview and Minewick, and that total property tax levies for 19x1 are as follows:

Monominee County	$100,000	50%
Crestview	40,000	20%
Minewick	60,000	30%
	$200,000	100%

A Tax Collection Agency Fund should be created. The county's custodial responsibility for collecting the taxes is recorded:

Taxes Receivable for Local Government Units	200,000	
Liability to Monominee County		100,000
Liability to Crestview		40,000
Liability to Minewick		60,000
To record fiduciary responsibility for tax collection		

If $170,000 of the levy is collected and $150,000 is remitted to the respective units of government during 19x1, the collection and remittance is recorded as follows:

Cash	170,000	
Taxes Receivable for Local Governmental Units		170,000
To record collection of taxes receivable		
Liability to Monominee County	90,000	
Liability to Crestview	35,000	
Liability to Minewick	25,000	
Cash		150,000
To record remittance of taxes collected		

If Monominee County charges Crestview and Minewick a fee of 1% of taxes collected, the total charges would be $700 ($70,000 collected for Crestview and Minewick times 1% = $700). Let us say that out of the $170,000 collected, $100,000 was for Monominee County, $40,000 for Crestview, and $30,000 for Minewick.

Then the collection fees would be recorded as follows:

Liability to Crestview	400	
Liability to Minewick	300	
Due to General Fund of Monominee County		700
To charge the towns of Crestview and Minewick a		
1% fee for taxes collected for them		

9.12 Financial Reporting Required of Governmental Units

When a governmental unit has more than one fund of a given type, the individual statements for that type of fund are usually combined for external reporting purposes. The statements for each type of fund are presented in combined financial statements for external reporting with separate columns for each type of fund. Combined statements may or may not contain total columns. In this manner, the number of financial statements required for external financial reporting in accordance with generally accepted accounting principles is reduced to the following:

71

1. A combined balance sheet for all fund types and account groups
2. A combined statement of revenues, expenditures, and changes in fund balances for all governmental fund types
3. A combined statement of revenues, expenditures, and changes in fund balances — budget and actual — for general and special revenue fund types
4. A combined statement of revenues, expenses, and changes in retained earnings for all proprietary fund types
5. A combined statement of changes in financial position for all proprietary fund types

Chapter Nine Review Questions

1. Is the Governmental Accounting Standards Board a public or a private organization?

Private.

2. What fund records all financial resources that are not accounted for in other funds?

The General Fund.

3. What is meant by the Modified Accrual Method of Accounting?

Most revenues are put down on the books when the cash is collected, but property taxes are accrued at the time they are levied. So property taxes use the accrual basis of accounting and most other entries use the cash basis.

4. When is an encumbrance recorded?

When a purchase order is approved by the city.

5. When an asset, such as a fire truck, is purchased by the city, is an asset debited or is an expense debited?

In municipal accounting, an expense account is usually debited.

6. What type of account is Investments?

Investments is a long-term asset account.

7. If the city government receives a donation of land from private sources or from the state or federal government, is it recorded on the city books at cost or at fair market value?

At fair market value at the time of receipt.

8. *Do governments, such as city, county and state governments, usually record depreciation on their fixed assets, such as buildings?*

No.

CHAPTER 10

ACCOUNTING FOR NONPROFIT ORGANIZATIONS

10.1 Accounting for Universities, Hospitals, and Voluntary Health and Welfare Organizations

The American Institute of Certified Public Accountants has issued Industry Audit Guides for Colleges & Universities, for Hospitals, and for Voluntary Health and Welfare Organizations.

Financial Accounting Standards Board Statement No. 32 discusses Specialized Accounting and Reporting Principles and Practices on Accounting and Auditing Matters for these three types of organizations.

These organizations are *alike* in that they are nonprofit, have service objectives, and use fund accounting practices.

These organizations *differ* in service objectives, sources of financing, and degree of autonomy.

10.2 College and University Accounting

Educational services are frequently financed, at least in part, without reference to those receiving the benefits. Accounting emphasis lies in showing the *sources* from which resources have been received and the *utilization* of those resources. *Fund Accounting* is used to achieve this.

10.2.1 Fund Groupings

Current Funds

1. *Unrestricted Current Funds* — Economic resources expendable for instruction, research, extension, and public service (residence halls, food service, athletics, college stores, student unions).

2. *Restricted Current Funds* — Economic resources expendable for operating purposes but restricted by donors or other outside agencies for a specific purpose.

Loan Funds — Money to be lent to students or faculty. Accounting must enable the sources and the restrictions to be identified.

Endowment and Similar Funds

1. *Endowment Funds* — Accounts for resources received from donors and outside agencies where the principal is maintained in perpetuity and the income is expended for general or specified purposes or added to principal.

2. *Term Endowment Funds* — Accounts for resources received from donors or outside agencies where the principal may be expended after some time period or event.

3. *Quasi-Endowment Funds* — Resources designated by the governing board (internal) to be invested indefinitely with the income being spent as directed.

Annuity and Life Income Funds

1. *Annuity Funds* — The college or university makes stipulated periodic payments from the fund to individuals as provided by the agreement with the donor.

2. *Life Income Funds* — Funds have been donated to the college or university with the requirement that the income from the funds be paid (usually until death) to a designated individual.

Plant Funds

1. *Unexpended Plant Funds* — Unexpended resources to be used to buy physical property.

2. *Renewal and Replacement Funds* — Resources to be used to renew or replace existing property.

3. *Retirement of Indebtedness Funds* — Resources set aside for debt service and debt retirements relating to institutional property.

4. *Investment in Plant Funds* — Accounting for land, buildings, other improvements and equipment and books, and liabilities relating to plant assets.

Agency Funds — Resources held by college or university of custodian for student or faculty groups.

10.2.2 General Accounting and Reporting Matters

Budgets are encouraged but not required.

Basic financial statements for colleges and universities

1. Combined Balance Sheet
2. Combined Statement of Changes in Fund Balances
3. Statement of Revenues, Expenditures, and Other Changes for the Current Funds' Grouping

Classifications

1. Revenues are classified by Source.
2. Expenditures are classified by Function.

Other Matters

1. Accrual Accounting is used.
2. Depreciation expense is not reported in the Statement of Current Funds Revenues, Expenditures, and Other Changes.
3. Expenditures for plant asset replacements and renewals are reported as current fund expenditures when acquired directly through current funds.

10.2.3 Current Funds, Loan Funds, and Endowment Funds

Current Funds — Only resources expendable for operating purposes. (These current funds are either unrestricted or restricted.)

1. *Restricted Funds* — The revenue of current restricted funds for a period is equal to current restricted fund expenditures for that period.

   Revenue of auxiliary enterprises (storerooms, motor pools, print shops) is normally kept on a cost reimbursement basis and no revenues or expenditures are recorded. Instead, the cost is reflected in the expenditures of the department or divisions receiving the goods and services.

2. *Revenue of Unrestricted Current Funds* — unrestricted gifts, grants, state appropriations, unrestricted earnings — but it *does not include* net capital gains of endowment funds. These must be accounted for in those funds themselves.

3. *Statement of Current Funds Revenues, Expenditures, and Other Changes*

MORNINGSIDE COLLEGE
STATEMENT OF CURRENT FUNDS REVENUES,
EXPENDITURES, AND OTHER CHANGES
For the Year Ended June 30, 19x3

	Unrestricted	Restricted	Total
REVENUES:			
Tuition and Fees	$ 900,000	$	$ 900,000
State Appropriations	300,000		300,000
Federal Grants & Contracts	20,000	10,000	30,000
Private Grants and Gifts	40,000	300,000	340,000
Endowment Income	35,000	21,000	56,000
Sales & Services of			
Educational Departments	3,000		3,000
Sales & Services of Auxiliary			
Enterprises	70,000		70,000
Total Current Revenues	$1,368,000	$ 331,000	$1,699,000
EXPENDITURES & MANDATORY TRANSFERS:			
Educational and General:			
Instruction	950,000	320,800	1,270,800
Research	400	200	600
Public Service & Extension	100		100
Student Services	9,000		9,000
Libraries	10,000		10,000
Operation & Maintenance of Plant	8,000		8,000
Scholarships & Grants	1,000	10,000	11,000
General Administration	7,000		7,000
Total Educational and			
General Expenditures	$ 985,500	$ 331,000	$1,316,500

10.2.4 Annuity and Life Income Funds

Annuity Funds

1. Assets are the actual cash or other asset investment.
2. Liabilities are debts related to fund assets and the actuarial amount of annuities payable.

MANDATORY TRANSFERS:			
Principal and Interest	8,000		8,000
Renewals & Replacements	2,000		2,000
Loan Fund Matching Grants	500		500
Total Educational & General	$ 996,000	$ 331,000	$1,327,000
AUXILIARY ENTERPRISES:			
Expenditures	15,000		15,000
Total Expenditures and			
Mandatory Transfers	$1,011,000	$ 331,000	$1,342,000
Net Increase (Decrease) in			
Fund Balances	$ 357,000	$ 0	$ 357,000

Life Income Funds

1. Assets are the actual cash or other asset investment.
2. Liabilities are debts related to fund assets and life income payments currently due.

10.2.5 Plant and Agency Funds

Plant Funds — Resources held for additions and improvements of the physical plant, or to renew or replace the physical plant, investments for future debt retirement.

Physical Plant includes land, buildings, and other improvements, and equipment.

Agency Funds — Accounting for assets held by the university for individual students and faculty members. These transactions affect only asset and liability accounts, not revenue or expense accounts.

10.2.6 Financial Statements

The Balance Sheet, Statement of Changes in Fund Balances, and Statement of Current Funds Revenues, Expenditures, and Other Changes make up the Financial Statements. These are often presented in columnar format.

10.3 Hospital Accounting

Hospital Accounting must follow generally accepted accounting principles.

Accounting and reporting standards are covered in the American Institute of Certified Public Accountants' *Audits of Providers of Health Care Services*, issued in 1990.

10.3.1 Fund Groupings

Unrestricted Funds — All unrestricted resources of the hospital as well as board-designated funds, those unrestricted resources that the governing board has set aside for specific purposes.

Restricted Funds

1. *Specific Purpose Funds* — Resources restricted by donors for specific operating purposes.

2. *Plant Replacement and Expansion Funds* — Accounting for donor-restricted resources such as property, plant, and equipment and revenue.

3. *Endowment Funds* — Accounting for resources restricted by donors to pure endowments or term endowments.

10.3.2 Accrual Accounting

Accrual Accounting must be used.

Hospitals measure and report revenues and expenses (rather than expenditures).

Hospitals use *cost* principles in measuring values of assets.

Hospitals *depreciate* plant assets.

Depreciation on minor equipment is determined on an inventory basis rather than by applying a depreciation formula.

10.3.3 Revenues and Expenses

Revenues

1. *Patient Service Revenues* — Routine care, nursing, delivery and labor rooms, emergency rooms, recovery rooms, medical supplies, laboratory, radiation, pharmacy, anesthesiology, physical therapy, respiratory therapy, speech therapy, ambulance.

2. *Other Operating Revenues* — Tuition from education programs, research and specific purpose grants, rental revenue, gift shop, television rental, telephone income, cafeteria income.

3. *Nonoperating Revenues* — Unrestricted gifts and grants, unrestricted income from endowments, investment income, gains from unrestricted funds, gains on sale of plant assets.

Expenses

1. Nursing services, laboratory expense, radiology, anesthesiology, pharmacy expense.

2. *General Services* — Housekeeping, maintenance, laundry.

3. *Physical Services* — Accounting, cashier, credits and collections, data processing.

4. *Administrative Services* — Personnel, purchasing, insurance, interest, governing board.

5. *Contra-Revenue Accounts* — Charity Allowances for the poor, Courtesy Allowances that are discounts for doctors and employees, Contractual Adjustments with Medicare and Blue Cross for reimbursement at less than established rates.

10.3.4 Financial Reporting

Financial Reporting includes the Balance sheets, Statement of Revenues and Expenses, Statements of Changes in Fund Balances, and Statements of Changes in Financial Position.

An example of Statement of Revenue and Expenses, and an example of Statement of Changes in Fund Balances appear on the following pages.

10.4 Voluntary Health and Welfare Organizations

Voluntary Health and Welfare Organizations are nonprofit entities supported by the public and providing voluntary services. The accounting standards for these organizations are provided by the 1974 Industry Audit Guide of the American Institute of Certified Public Accountants entitled, Audits of Voluntary Health and Welfare Organizations.

Purpose of this accounting is to disclose how the entity's resources have been acquired and used to accomplish the objectives of the organization.

ST. LUKE'S HOSPITAL
STATEMENT OF REVENUES AND EXPENSES
For the Year Ended December 31, 19X3

Patient Service Revenues		
Inpatient Services	$6,000,000	
Outpatient Services	1,400,000	
Total Patient Service Revenues		$7,400,000
Deduct:		
Medicare Contractual Allowances	300,000	
Employee Allowances	1,000	
Charity Allowances	13,000	
Provision for Uncollectible Accounts	100,000	414,000
Net Patient Service Revenues		6,986,000
Other Operating Revenues		1,000
Total Operating Revenues		6,987,000
Operating Expenses		
Nursing Services	2,600,000	
Other Professional Services	1,400,000	
General Services	1,200,000	
Fiscal Services	300,000	
Administrative Services	150,000	
Provisions for Depreciation	200,000	
Total Operating Expenses	$ 5,850,000	−5,850,000
Income from Operations		$1,137,000

10.4.1 Fund Accounting

Fund Accounting is used to segregate restricted and unrestricted resources.

Current Unrestricted Funds — Accounts for resources expendable at the discretion of the governing board.

Current Restricted Funds — Accounts for resources expendable for current uses, but restricted by donors for specific operating purposes.

81

ST. LUKE'S HOSPITAL
STATEMENT OF CHANGES IN FUND BALANCES
For the Year Ended December 31, 19X3

UNRESTRICTED FUNDS

Operating Fund

Fund Balance, January 1, 19x3	$1,200,000	
Excess Revenues over Expenses	1,500,000	
Transfers to Plant Replacement and Expansion Funds (third-party restrictions)	(100,000)	
Transfer from Plant Replacement and Expansion Funds	200,000	
Fund Balance, December 31, 19x3		$2,800,000

Board-Designated Funds

Fund Balance, January 1, 19x3	$ 120,000	
Investment Income	15,000	
Transfer to Operating Fund (nonoperating revenues)	(30,000)	105,000
Total Unrestricted Fund Balances December 31, 19x3		$2,905,000

RESTRICTED FUNDS

Specific Purpose Funds

Fund Balance, January 1, 19x3	$ 320,000
Restricted Gifts and Grants	70,000
Transfer to Operating Fund (other operating revenues)	(30,000)
Income from Investments	10,000
Fund Balance, December 31, 19x3	$ 370,000

Plant Replacement and Expansion Funds

Fund Balance, January 1, 19x3	$ 331,000
Income from Investments	60,000
Transfer to Operating Fund for Equipment Purchase	(200,000)
Transfer from Operating Fund to reflect third-party restrictions	150,000
Fund Balance, December 31, 19x3	$ 341,000

Endowment Funds

Fund Balance, January 1, 19x3	$3,000,000
Additions to Term Endowments	60,000
Fund Balance, December 31, 19x3	$3,060,000

Land, Building and Equipment Funds — Accounts for the net investment in plant assets and unexpended resources restricted by donors to acquisition or replacement of plant assets. Liabilities related to plant assets are also included.

Endowment Funds — Accounts for gifts and bequests under endowment agreements with donors.

Custodial Funds — Accounts for assets received and to be held or distributed on instructions of the person or entity from whom received.

Loan and Annuity Funds — Accounts for resources restricted by agreements with donors for loans or annuities.

10.4.2 Support and Revenue

Earnings for voluntary health and welfare organizations are made up of support and revenue.

Cash Donations and Pledges — The chief income for these groups.

Donated Securities — Recorded at fair market value as of the date of gift.

Donated Materials and Services

1. Donated materials are recorded at their fair values when received.
2. Donated services are usually not reported, unless they are controlled by the organization, clearly measurable, and would otherwise be performed by salaried personnel.

Investment Income and Realized Gains and Losses — Reported under Restricted Revenue or Unrestricted Revenue, as the case may be.

10.4.3 Expenses

Expenses are classified as Program Services and Supporting Services.

Program Services — Expenses incurred in providing the organization's social service activities.

Expenses (Program Services) — Research, public education, professional education, community services, patient services.

Supporting Services — Expenses for administration and fundraising.

10.4.4 Financial Reporting

Basic Financial Statements include Statement of Support, Revenues, and Expenses; Statement of Functional Expenses; and the Balance Sheet.

Chapter Ten Review Questions

1. Why is university accounting somewhat different from accounting for a regular business?

In a regular business, benefits are usually received by those who pay for the goods or services. In university accounting, educational services are frequently financed, at least in part, without reference to those receiving the benefits.

2. What is the difference between restricted funds and unrestricted funds?

Restricted funds can only be spent for uses designated by boards or donors. On the other hand, unrestricted funds can be spent as needed.

3. What is an Endowment Fund?

Resources received from donors and outside agencies where the principal is maintained in perpetuity and the income from the investment is spent for specified purposes or added to the principal.

4. How does a Term Endowment Fund differ from an Endowment Fund?

Endowment funds are usually perpetual while a term endowment fund ends after a certain specified period or after the happening of a certain event.

5. What is an Annuity Fund?

One where the university makes periodic payments from the fund to individuals according to an agreement.

6. What are Life Income Funds?

Persons donate money to the university and this money is invested. Income from the invested money is paid periodically to the donor. Upon the donor's death, the invested money is used by the university.

7. What are Plant Funds?

Monies used to buy new property for the university or to renew or replace existing property.

8. *Are budgets required in university accounting?*

   No, but they are recommended.

9. *What is the main difference between an Income Statement of a business and a Statement of Current Funds Revenues, Expenditures, and Other Changes for a university?*

   The university statement is segregated between restricted and unrestricted funds.

10. *How does hospital accounting differ from university accounting?*

   Hospitals must use accrual accounting, value assets at cost, and depreciate plant assets. On the other hand, universities usually use fund accounting, can value assets as they wish, and do not need to depreciate plant assets.

"The ESSENTIALS" of
ACCOUNTING & BUSINESS

Each book in the Accounting and Business ESSENTIALS series offers all essential information about the subject it covers. It includes every important principle and concept, and is designed to help students in preparing for exams and doing homework. The Accounting and Business ESSENTIALS are excellent supplements to any class text or course of study.

The Accounting and Business ESSENTIALS are complete and concise, with quick access to needed information. They also provide a handy reference source at all times. The Accounting and Business ESSENTIALS are prepared with REA's customary concern for high professional quality and student needs.

Available titles include:

Accounting I & II

Advanced Accounting I & II

Advertising

Auditing

Business Law I & II

Business Statistics I & II

College & University Writing

Corporate Taxation

Cost & Managerial Accounting I & II

Financial Management

Income Taxation

Intermediate Accounting I & II

Macroeconomics I & II

Marketing Principles

Microeconomics

Money & Banking I & II

If you would like more information about any of these books,
complete the coupon below and return it to us or go to your local bookstore.